NEW MEXICO

The Land of Enchantment

BY
JOHN HAMILTON

Abdo & Daughters

An imprint of Abdo Publishing | abdopublishing.com

abdopublishing.com

Published by ABDO Publishing, a division of ABDO, PO Box 398166, Minneapolis, Minnesota 55439. Copyright © 2017 by Abdo Consulting Group, Inc. International copyrights reserved in all countries. No part of this book may be reproduced in any form without written permission from the publisher. ABDO & Daughters™ is a trademark and logo of ABDO Publishing.

Printed in the United States of America, North Mankato, Minnesota.
042016
092016

Editor: Sue Hamilton   **Contributing Editor:** Bridget O'Brien
Graphic Design: Sue Hamilton
Cover Art Direction: Candice Keimig   **Cover Photo Selection:** Neil Klinepier
Cover Photo: iStock
Interior Images: Alamy, Albuquerque Isotopes, AP, Bureau of Land Management, Dreamstime, Duke City Gladiators, Eric Grunwald, Getty, Granger, Henry Farny (artist), History in Full Color-Restoration/Colorization, Intel Corporation, iStock, John Hamilton, Mile High Maps, Minden Pictures, NASA, National Park Service, New Mexico Aggies, New Mexico Lobos, New Mexico Stars, New Mexico State Government, Roswell Invaders, Santa Fe Fuego, Science Source, University of New Mexico Sports, White Sands Pupfish, & Wikimedia.

Statistics: *State and City Populations*, U.S. Census Bureau, July 1, 2015/2014 estimates; *Land and Water Area*, U.S. Census Bureau, 2010 Census, MAF/TIGER database; *State Temperature Extremes*, NOAA National Climatic Data Center; *Climatology and Average Annual Precipitation*, NOAA National Climatic Data Center, 1980-2015 statewide averages; *State Highest and Lowest Points*, NOAA National Geodetic Survey.

Websites: To learn more about the United States, visit booklinks.abdopublishing.com. These links are routinely monitored and updated to provide the most current information available.

Cataloging-in-Publication Data

Names: Hamilton, John, 1959- author.
Title: New Mexico / by John Hamilton.
Description: Minneapolis, MN : Abdo Publishing, [2017] | Series: The United
    States of America | Includes index.
Identifiers: LCCN 2015957623 | ISBN 9781680783339 (lib. bdg.) |
    ISBN 9781680774375 (ebook)
Subjects: LCSH: New Mexico--Juvenile literature.
Classification: DDC 978.9--dc23
LC record available at http://lccn.loc.gov/2015957623

CONTENTS

THE LAND OF ENCHANTMENT

New Mexico is a state of unexpected adventure. There are scorching deserts and dusty country roads. But there are also snow-capped mountains, flat-topped mesas, green forests, and breathtaking sunsets. The air smells of sage and piñon pine. Colors abound, from earth-toned adobe houses to the swirling skirts in traditional dance fiestas.

The state's culture is a mix of Anglo-American, Hispanic, and Native American traditions. First settled by pueblo-dwelling Native Americans, the land was claimed by Spanish treasure seekers and settlers starting in the 1500s, decades before the *Mayflower* brought Pilgrims to New England.

Today, New Mexico is a mix of old and new, tied together with a love of adventure, sunny days, and roasted chile peppers. Authentic Old West culture lives side-by-side with modern life, which includes bustling cities, artist colonies, and high-technology research labs. New Mexico truly is a land of enchantment.

Young people perform a Mexican folk dance in the village of Mesilla, near Las Cruces, New Mexico.

An enchanting desert morning near Santa Fe, New Mexico.

QUICK FACTS

Name: The first explorers of the state considered the land to be a northern addition to Mexico.

State Capital: Santa Fe, population 70,297

Date of Statehood: January 6, 1912 (47th state)

Population: 2,085,109 (36th-most populous state)

Area (Total Land and Water): 121,590 square miles (314,917 sq km), 5th-largest state

Largest City: Albuquerque, population 557,169

Nickname: Land of Enchantment

Motto: *Crescit Eundo* (It Grows As It Goes)

State Bird: Roadrunner

State Flower: Yucca

State Gemstone: Turquoise

State Tree: Piñon Pine

State Song: "O Fair New Mexico"

Highest Point: Wheeler Peak, 13,161 feet (4,011 m)

Lowest Point: Red Bluff Reservoir, 2,842 feet (866 m)

Average July High Temperature: 88°F (31°C)

Record High Temperature: 122°F (50°C), near Carlsbad on June 27, 1994

Average January Low Temperature: 21°F (-6°C)

Record Low Temperature: -50°F (-46°C), at Gavilan on February 1, 1951

Average Annual Precipitation: 14 inches (36 cm)

Number of U.S. Senators: 2

Number of U.S. Representatives: 3

U.S. Postal Service Abbreviation: NM

QUICK FACTS

GEOGRAPHY

New Mexico is in the Southwest region of the United States. It is the fifth-largest state, covering 121,590 square miles (314,917 sq km). Much of the land is arid desert, but there are also forested mountains, plains, flat-topped mesas, canyons, and river valleys.

New Mexico is nearly square shaped. The state's longest and most important river is the Rio Grande. It flows from north to south through the middle of the state. Many of New Mexico's biggest cities are located along or near the river. Other important rivers include the Pecos, Canadian, San Juan, and Gila Rivers. New Mexico's largest body of water is the Elephant Butte Reservoir in the south-central part of the state.

The Rio Grande flows through the city of Albuquerque, New Mexico.

New Mexico's total land and water area is 121,590 square miles (314,917 sq km). It is the fifth-largest state. The state capital is Santa Fe.

Much of the eastern third of New Mexico is covered by arid plains. The land is mostly flat grasslands. Large parts of the plains are used to graze cattle and sheep, thanks to the blue grama grass that grows in the soil. It is the official state grass of New Mexico.

The Basin and Range Province occupies much of southern New Mexico. It is a series of flat, dry desert valleys that alternate with steep mountain ranges, most of which run north and south. The dry, bowl-like valleys are called basins. The largest is Tularosa Basin. It is located between the San Andres and Sacramento Mountains.

The southernmost part of the Rocky Mountains is in northeastern and north-central New Mexico. East of the Rio Grande are the Sangre de Cristo Mountains. They are home to Wheeler Peak, the tallest point in the state. Its summit soars to 13,161 feet (4,011 m).

New Mexico shares its northwestern corner with three other states—Arizona, Utah, and Colorado. Visitors like to come to the Four Corners so they can stand on four states at once.

The Colorado Plateau is in the northwestern corner of New Mexico. The barren desert land is filled with canyons, cliffs, and mesas. One famous landmark is Shiprock. It is the core of an ancient volcano that juts up from the surrounding flat ground. It was exposed by millions of years of erosion.

Shiprock

CLIMATE AND
WEATHER

Temperatures in New Mexico are usually mild, although they vary greatly depending on the season and elevation. It is usually cooler in the mountains. The average statewide high temperature in July is 88°F (31°C). The highest temperature ever recorded in the state occurred on June 27, 1994, just east of the city of Carlsbad. On that day, the temperature rose to a sweltering 122°F (50°C). In January, the average low temperature is 21°F (-6°C). On February 1, 1951, at Gavilan, the thermometer sank to a bone-chilling -50°F (-46°C), a record low for the state.

Lightning flashes in the sky in Roswell, New Mexico.

Residents of Farmington, New Mexico, watch flash flood waters race down the Animas River after a heavy rainfall struck northeast of the town.

Much of New Mexico has a dry desert climate. Statewide, the average annual precipitation is just 14 inches (36 cm). There is more rain on the eastern plains than the deserts of the west. The mountains of northern New Mexico receive more rain and snow.

Sometimes the rain pours so hard that dry soil can't absorb all the water. Dangerous flash floods can occur. Lightning strikes are also common. During dry spells in the desert, the wind sometimes gathers loose soil and spins it into funnel-shaped clouds. These usually harmless whirlwinds are called dust devils.

CLIMATE AND WEATHER

PLANTS AND
ANIMALS

New Mexico mainly has a desert climate, but there are many ecosystems in the state, from plains to forested mountains to river valleys. Forests and woodlands cover approximately 22 million acres (8.9 million ha) of land, which is about 28 percent of the state. Many of New Mexico's forests grow on the sides of mountains, where it is cooler and wetter. These "sky islands" provide more shelter for plants and wildlife than the arid deserts and plains that surround the mountains.

A Cooper's hawk flies over quaking aspens in Santa Fe National Forest, in New Mexico's Sangre de Cristo Mountains.

A bighorn sheep stands in patches of sagebrush in Río Grande del Norte National Monument, north of Taos, New Mexico, near the Colorado border.

Trees common to New Mexico include piñon pine, aspen, cottonwood, spruce, juniper, fir, and ponderosa pine. Piñon pine is the official state tree. It grows between 10 to 30 feet (3 to 9 m) tall, and has a sweet, woodsy fragrance that is beloved by state residents and visitors alike.

On the arid plains and deserts of New Mexico, the plants that thrive do not require much water. They include blue and black grama grasses, creosote bushes, sagebrush, saltbush, mesquite, and cacti.

PLANTS AND ANIMALS

Common animals found in New Mexico, especially in cooler mountain areas with more water, include mule deer, bighorn sheep, elk, foxes, cougars, porcupines, squirrels, opossums, skunks, minks, bats, muskrats, coyotes, and bobcats. Several species of trout are found swimming in mountain streams and rivers.

In New Mexico's deserts and plains areas, animals have adapted to live with less water. They include jackrabbits, pronghorn antelopes, prairie dogs, and kangaroo rats.

The Mexican gray wolf was once common in New Mexico, but overhunting nearly eliminated it. In recent years, small numbers of wolves have been reintroduced. Their familiar howl can once again be heard in the remote forests of Gila National Forest in southwestern New Mexico.

A jackrabbit's big ears are designed to help it cool down. The blood vessels running through the ears dissipate its body heat.

The official state reptile is the New Mexico whiptail lizard.

There are many kinds of snakes, lizards, and turtles living in New Mexico. They include collared lizards, banded geckos, Gila monsters, and horned lizards. The official state reptile is the New Mexico whiptail lizard.

There are 46 snake species in New Mexico. Eight are venomous, including several kinds of rattlesnakes and one species of coral snake. Snakes mainly eat small animals such as mice and birds.

There are more than 540 species of birds found in New Mexico. They include great horned owls, red-tailed hawks, bald eagles, western bluebirds, crows, and meadowlarks. The roadrunner is the official state bird. They can often be seen scampering across the desert at speeds up to 20 miles per hour (32 kph).

HISTORY

Long before Europeans arrived, the first people to settle the New Mexico area appeared at least 11,000 years ago, possibly much earlier. These Paleo-Indians were the ancestors of today's Native Americans. In time, they developed into what is called the Clovis culture. They used stone spear points and other tools to hunt big game such as mammoths, bison, and elk.

Later, Native Americans in the New Mexico area included members of the Anasazi culture, also called the Ancestral Puebloans. They first appeared approximately 2,000 to 3,500 years ago, and lived in New Mexico for hundreds of years. They grew corn and made pottery and woven baskets. Anasazi is a Navajo Native American word that means "ancient ones" or "ancient enemy." They built multi-room dwellings, often into the sides of sheer cliffs. These structures are called pueblos. They helped protect the Anasazi from enemies. Many pueblo ruins can be seen today in New Mexico.

Eventually, the Ancestral Puebloans left the region, perhaps because of warfare or a long drought. They scattered and formed smaller groups of Pueblo peoples. In time, other Native American groups also settled in the New Mexico region. They included Apache, Navajo, and Ute Indians.

Ancestral Puebloans lived in cliff dwellings, such as the ones still seen in Bandelier, New Mexico.

The first European explorers came to the New Mexico area in the early 1500s. At that time, New Mexico was a remote province of Mexico, which was ruled by Spain. In 1540, Spanish explorer Francisco Vázquez de Coronado led hundreds of conquistadors into the desert Southwest. They were looking for the mythical Seven Golden Cities of Cibola. They discovered the Grand Canyon, the Colorado River, and even ventured as far as the Great Plains in present-day Kansas. Many Native American tribes were encountered, but the conquistadors found no gold. The Native Americans got something better than gold: horses left behind by the Spaniards. They used them to travel, and to make hunting easier.

In 1610, Spanish rulers made Santa Fe the capital of New Mexico. (Today, it is the oldest capital city in the United States.) Settlers began moving into the area.

In the late 1500s, Spain established El Camino Real de Tierra Adentro (The Royal Road of the Interior Land). The trade route ran from Mexico City to today's San Juan Pueblo, New Mexico.

Missionaries forced many Native Americans to change their religion and culture. In 1680, during the Pueblo Revolt, angry Native Americans pushed the Spanish out of New Mexico. But by 1692, the Spanish returned. They founded the city of Albuquerque in 1706. More Spanish settlers arrived to farm and raise sheep.

Mexico won independence from Spain in 1821. New Mexico was still a part of Mexico at the time. However, New Mexico had close ties with the United States. It traded goods such as wool, furs, and horses.

The United States and Mexico went to war in 1846. That year, United States Army General Stephen Kearny and his troops captured Santa Fe with no resistance. The Americans claimed all of New Mexico.

After the Mexican-American War (1846-1848), New Mexico became an official territory of the United States in 1850. By the late 1800s, cattle ranching had become an important industry in New Mexico.

Many Navajo and Apache Native Americans fought fiercely to hold back the tide of American settlers. They refused to be forced onto reservation lands. Led by warriors such as Cochise, Mangas Coloradas, Geronimo, and others, the Apache people fought in New Mexico and Arizona. They battled settlers and soldiers for about 35 years. The Apache Wars finally eased in 1886 after Geronimo's capture.

In the 1800s, Apache people fought fiercely in Arizona and New Mexico to hold onto their land.

The first atomic bomb test took place near Alamogordo, New Mexico, on July 16, 1945.

Despite many years of conflict, settlement continued in New Mexico, spurred on by mineral discoveries and by new farm irrigation methods. New Mexico became the 47th state to join the Union in 1912. Newly built railroads, roads, and automobiles fueled even more growth, especially in the cities.

During World War II (1939-1945), the United States Army built bases and secret research laboratories in the state. In 1945, the Los Alamos National Laboratory helped create the first atomic bomb. The first nuclear test blast took place at today's White Sands Missile Range on July 16, 1945.

In recent decades, New Mexico's population has rapidly expanded. Many people work on military bases and science laboratories. Agriculture, electronics, and mineral resources are strong industries in the state. New Mexico's natural beauty attracts artists and writers. The state has also grown a reputation as a good place to retire, thanks to its clear, healthy mountain air.

HISTORY

DID YOU KNOW?

• The St. James Hotel in Cimarron, New Mexico, was built in 1872 along the Santa Fe Trail. It may also be the most haunted place in the West. During its heyday, many famous lawmen and outlaws stayed at the St. James, including Wyatt Earp, Buffalo Bill Cody, and Jesse James. Gunfights often erupted in the hotel's saloon, or in private card games upstairs. Bullet holes can still be seen in the saloon's tin ceiling. Several people were murdered over the years. Their spirits, some people swear, haunt the hallways and rooms of the hotel to this day. Creepy Room 18 has frightened so many people it is kept permanently locked and no longer rented out to guests. Is it a restless ghost that haunts Room 18? Or imaginations running wild? Whether or not the St. James harbors phantoms, it is a placed filled with authentic Western history, and is listed on the National Register of Historic Places.

• The Santa Fe Trail was a route used by pioneers in the 1800s traveling westward across the country. It was also used by wagon trains to transport goods back and forth between large eastern cities and the frontier. The trail started in Missouri, then wound its way across the Great Plains until ending near Santa Fe, New Mexico. Today, parts of the trail are identified as a National Scenic Byway. In some parts of New Mexico, the ruts from the thousands of wagons that moved along the trail are still visible on the landscape.

• Tumbleweeds are very common in the deserts of New Mexico, but they are not native plants. They were accidentally brought to America by Ukrainian farmers in the 1800s. The seeds hitchhiked in  containers of flax seed and other grains. Tumbleweeds have many nicknames, including "Russian thistle." When the shrubs dry out, they detach from their roots. The prickly pests roll across the windswept landscape, dropping their seeds (as many as 250,000 per plant!) Today, they are a symbol of the West, but they can also cause big headaches. Sometimes, so many tumbleweeds accumulate in people's yards that bulldozers are needed to clear them out.

PEOPLE

William H. Bonney (1859-1881) was the gunfighter outlaw known as Billy the Kid. Born in New York City, New York, his real name was Henry McCarty. He grew up in New Mexico before it was a state. He was a murderer who became famous for gambling, stealing horses and cattle, and for joining a gang of outlaws in New Mexico. He twice escaped from jail and the death penalty. Legends say he killed 21 men, one for each year of his life, but that is almost certainly an exaggeration. Bonney was on the run in New Mexico and Arizona, always one step ahead of the law, until his luck finally ran out. In 1881, he was tracked down and shot dead by Sheriff Pat Garrett at Fort Sumner, New Mexico.

Maria Martinez (1887-1980) was a Native American artist who was born and grew up in San Ildefonso Pueblo in north-central New Mexico. She was most famous for her pottery. It was made in the traditional style of the ancient Pueblo peoples, which was glossy jet-black ceramic with lighter black designs. She learned how to make pottery from her aunt when she was growing up.

Tony Hillerman (1925-2008) wrote best-selling mystery and detective novels set in New Mexico. His books featured police officers Joe Leaphorn and Jim Chee of the Navajo Tribal Police (called the Navajo Nation Police today). He won many honors for his work, including an Edgar Allan Poe Award from the Mystery Writers of America. Hillerman spent much of his adult life in Albuquerque, New Mexico.

Neil Patrick Harris (1973-) is a film, stage, and television actor. He has starred in dozens of productions, but he is best known for his role as Barney Stinson in the long-running television comedy *How I Met Your Mother*. He has also hosted several awards shows, including the Emmy Awards and the Academy Awards. Harris was born in Albuquerque, New Mexico.

Holly Holm (1981-) is a mixed martial artist and former boxer. She has won multiple boxing world titles, but the southpaw's most famous fight was at UFC 193 on November 15, 2015. During the mixed martial arts women's bantamweight championship match, Holm handed heavily favored Ronda Rousey her first loss with a knockout kick. Holm was born in Albuquerque, New Mexico.

Nancy Lopez (1957-) is a professional golfer who has won more than 50 pro tournaments. In 1978, during her first full season as a professional golfer, she won nine tournaments (five consecutively). That achievement earned her the Ladies Professional Golf Association (LPGA) Rookie of the Year Award. She was inducted into the LPGA Hall of Fame in 1987. Lopez grew up in Roswell, New Mexico.

Jeff Bezos (1964-) is an e-commerce pioneer who founded Amazon.com. He loved computers at an early age. In 1986, he earned degrees in electrical science and computer science from New Jersey's Princeton University. After graduation, he worked for an investment firm in New York City, New York. In 1995, after moving to Seattle, Washington, he started Amazon from an office in his garage. Today, it is one of the biggest e-commerce sites in the world. Bezos was born in Albuquerque, New Mexico.

CITIES

Albuquerque is the largest city in New Mexico. Its population is approximately 557,169. It is located along the banks of the Rio Grande, in the central part of the state. Founded in 1706 as a farming community, the city is named after a Spanish duke. Today, Albuquerque is the industrial center of the state. There are many advanced technology companies in the city, including Sandia National Laboratories and Intel Corporation. The University of New Mexico enrolls more than 27,000 students. The university is one of Albuquerque's top employers, along with Kirtland Air Force Base. The city has many museums, shops, and art galleries. Old Town Albuquerque has historic adobe buildings from the city's early days.

Santa Fe is the capital of New Mexico. Located in the north-central part of the state, its population is about 70,297. Founded in 1610, it is the oldest capital city in the United States. Santa Fe is known for its community of painters, sculptors, and writers. A favorite tourist destination, people come to the city for its beautiful mountain landscapes, colorful sunsets, and rich cultural heritage. There are many adobe homes. Music lovers enjoy the Santa Fe Opera and the Santa Fe Ballet.

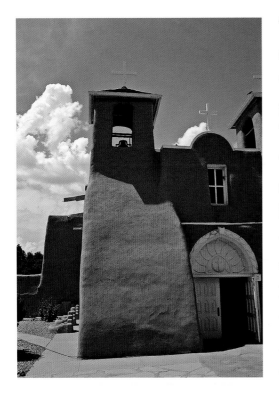

Taos is a small town in the Sangre de Cristo Mountains, 70 miles (113 km) northeast of Santa Fe. Its population is approximately 5,766. Taos Pueblo, just north of the city, was built more than 1,000 years ago. There are many other historic buildings in the city, including the San Francisco de Asis Mission Church, built in the early 1800s. Many artists and writers make their home in Taos. Photographer Ansel Adams and painter Georgia O'Keeffe both spent time in Taos.

Las Cruces is the second-largest city in New Mexico. Its population is about 101,408. Las Cruces is located in the south-central part of the state, near the border with Texas and Mexico. The city is in the fertile Mesilla Valley, a major agricultural area, thanks to irrigation. To the east of the city loom the beautiful Organ Mountains. New Mexico State University is located in Las Cruces. The defense industry, including the nearby White Sands Missile Range, is an important employer.

Rio Rancho is a medium-sized city in central New Mexico, just north of Albuquerque. Its population is approximately 93,820. It is the third-largest city in the state. It is also one of the fastest growing. One of the city's largest employers is Intel Corporation. It has a large computer microchip factory in the city. Other big employers include education, health care, and banking.

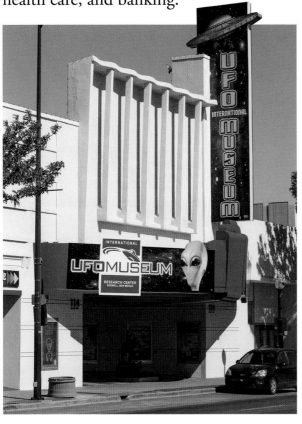

Roswell is the fifth-largest city in New Mexico. It is in the southeastern part of the state. Its population is about 48,608. It is an important regional farming center. There are many cattle and horse ranches in the area. Manufacturing and petroleum processing are also important. Roswell is most famous for being connected to an unidentified flying object (UFO) incident at a nearby military base in 1947.

TRANSPORTATION

Early in its history, New Mexico was an isolated place that was difficult to travel to. The 1,600-mile (2,575-km) long El Camino Real de Tierra Adentro Trail connected New Mexico with cities and markets in Mexico more than 300 years ago.

Today, New Mexico has 70,772 miles (113,896 km) of public roadways. Interstate I-40 travels east and west across the middle of the state. Interstate I-25 goes mostly north and south. On its northern section, it approximately follows the same path as the old Santa Fe Trail. Both interstates intersect with Albuquerque in the middle of the state.

New Mexico's major interstates intersect in Albuquerque, near the state's center.

Albuquerque International Sunport averages more than 124,000 takeoffs and landings a year. It is New Mexico's busiest airport.

New Mexico has a network of 1,837 miles (2,956 km) of railroad tracks that crisscross the state. The most common goods hauled are coal and food products, followed by chemicals, petroleum, and farm products. Passengers are served by Amtrak's Southwest Chief, which runs through Albuquerque. The Sunset Limited and Texas Eagle lines travel through the southwestern corner of the state.

New Mexico's busiest airport is Albuquerque International Sunport. It handles nearly five million passengers each year. There are dozens of smaller airports throughout the state.

NATURAL
RESOURCES

There are approximately 24,700 farms and ranches in New Mexico, with an average size of 1,749 acres (708 ha). The yearly market value of New Mexico's farm products is about $2.5 billion.

Beef cattle and sheep ranching are the biggest agricultural activities in New Mexico. Other livestock raised includes horses, goats, and chickens. The most important crops raised are hay, onions, chile peppers, corn, wheat, cotton, beans, and sorghum.

Ranchers herd cattle through New Mexico on their way to market.

New Mexico is famous for its chile peppers, which are the official state vegetable. Peppers get their spicy zing from the chemical capsaicin. They are an essential ingredient in Southwestern cooking. Many state residents hang bunches of peppers (called *ristras*) to dry in the open air outside their homes.

New Mexico is one of the nation's top producers of crude oil and natural gas. There are more than 2,000 oil and gas fields in the state. New Mexico is second in the nation for copper production, behind Arizona. Coal is also a big part of the state's mining industry. Other important minerals include gypsum (used in cement), molybdenum (for making steel), and potash (used in fertilizers).

Although New Mexico relies mainly on coal and natural gas for its energy needs, it ranks sixth in electricity generated from solar energy, thanks to the state's sunny skies.

A solar power station in New Mexico.

NATURAL RESOURCES

INDUSTRY

New Mexico's economy greatly depends on spending by the state and federal governments, especially the United States military. It provides approximately 25 percent of all jobs in the state.

There are several large military bases in New Mexico. Combined, they employ tens of thousands of state residents. The United States Air Force has three bases in New Mexico. Kirtland Air Force Base is in Albuquerque. Cannon Air Force Base is in eastern New Mexico, near the town of Clovis. Holloman Air Force Base is in south-central New Mexico, near the town of Alamogordo.

In addition to its Air Force bases, New Mexico is also home to the United States Army's White Sands Missile Range and a portion of Fort Bliss. There are also two large government scientific research labs that are major employers: Sandia National Laboratories and Los Alamos National Laboratory, where nuclear weapons are designed.

The U.S. Army's White Sands Missile Range has an open-air museum that draws hundreds of visitors each year. It features more than 50 missiles and rockets.

The Albuquerque International Balloon Fiesta is held each year in October. It is the world's largest hot-air balloon gathering, with hundreds of balloons. Upwards of 100,000 tourists visit Albuquerque's Balloon Fiesta Park to walk among the amazing balloons and watch them take flight.

New Mexico's factories make products such as computer and electrical equipment, petroleum products, food products, printing materials, furniture, and much more. Most manufacturing takes place in the Albuquerque area.

The service industry is a big part of New Mexico's economy, especially tourism. More than 30 million people visit the state each year, drawn by New Mexico's unique culture and breathtaking scenery. The tourism industry supports approximately 200,000 jobs in the state. Visitors spend more than $6 billion in New Mexico yearly.

INDUSTRY

SPORTS

There are no major league professional sports teams in New Mexico. The Albuquerque Isotopes are a Minor League Baseball team affiliated with the Colorado Rockies. There are also several smaller baseball teams in the state. They belong to the independent Pecos League. They include the Santa Fe Fuego, the Roswell Invaders, and the White Sands Pupfish. The Duke City Gladiators play indoor football in Albuquerque. The New Mexico Stars also play indoor football. Their home games are in Rio Rancho.

Albuquerque's University of New Mexico has popular sports teams called the Lobos. They have 9 men's and 11 women's teams, including football, baseball, track & field, and volleyball. New Mexico State University is in Las Cruces. The school's teams are called the Aggies.

A bull riding competition takes place at a rodeo in Galisteo, New Mexico.

Rodeo is a very popular sport in New Mexico, both at the high school and professional level. Events include bronc riding, steer wrestling, tie-down and team roping, barrel racing, and bull riding. The Lea County Fair & Rodeo is the largest contest in the state.

Fly fishing is very popular in the San Juan River below the Navajo Dam in northeastern New Mexico. Fishing, along with boating and scuba diving, is also popular at Elephant Butte Reservoir, in southern New Mexico. It is the state's largest body of water.

SPORTS

ENTERTAINMENT

The Fiestas de Santa Fe has been held each autumn for more than 300 years in the city of Santa Fe. The festival starts with a religious ceremony, followed by several days of food, music, and New Mexico Hispanic heritage. It includes a giant puppet called Zozobra, which represents the gloom and hardships of the previous year. When it is set on fire, it symbolizes the hope for a trouble-free new year.

The Albuquerque International Balloon Fiesta is the world's largest hot-air balloon gathering. For nine days each October, the skies over the city are filled with hundreds of colorful hot air balloons.

Zozobra, a giant puppet, represents hardships from the previous year. When it is set on fire during the Fiestas de Santa Fe, it symbolizes hope for the new year.

Each night, thousands of Mexican free-tailed bats fly out of Carlsbad Caverns.

Carlsbad Caverns National Park is in the Chihuahuan Desert of southeastern New Mexico. It contains the largest natural underground chamber in North America. Each night, hundreds of thousands of Mexican free-tailed bats exit the cave in search of food.

The Sandia Peak Tramway near Albuquerque is the second-longest passenger aerial tramway in the world. It ascends 3,819 feet (1,164 m) to the top of Sandia Mountain.

White Sands National Monument, with its massive gypsum dune fields, is located in Tularosa Basin in southern New Mexico.

The Shiprock Northern Navajo Nation Fair is a weeklong festival celebrating Navajo culture. It features parades, carnivals, crafts, rodeo contests, and pow-wows.

ENTERTAINMENT

TIMELINE

9000 BC—Paleo-Indians arrive in the New Mexico area.

1500 BC—The first Anasazi (Ancestral Puebloans) people appear in New Mexico. They build large cities into the sides of cliffs for protection.

1500s—Several Native American groups settle in the New Mexico area, including the Apache, Navajo, and Ute tribes.

1540—Spanish explorer Francisco Vázquez de Coronado leads an expedition into today's New Mexico looking for treasure.

1610—Spanish rulers make Santa Fe the capital of New Mexico.

1680—The Pueblo Revolt drives Spaniards out of New Mexico.

1692—Spanish forces return and begin taking back control of New Mexico.

1821—Mexico declares independence from Spain. New Mexico is no longer under Spanish rule, but remains a part of Mexico.

1846—The United States captures New Mexico during the Mexican-American War.

1849-1886—The Apache Wars are fought between the U.S. military and Native Americans who fight to keep their native lands.

1850—New Mexico becomes a United States territory.

1912—New Mexico becomes the 47th state.

1945—The U.S. military's Los Alamos National Laboratory helps develop the first atomic bomb. The bomb is tested at near Alamogordo.

1947—Rumors spread that soldiers recover the remains of a UFO near the city of Roswell.

1940-1960—New Mexico's population doubles. There is massive United States government spending on Air Force bases, missile ranges, and science laboratories.

1980—Intel Corporation opens a large semiconductor fabrication factory in Rio Rancho, spurring rapid job and population growth.

2011—Susana Martinez takes office as the first female governor of New Mexico. She is also the first Hispanic female governor in the United States.

2015—The University of New Mexico Lobos women's cross-country team wins the NCAA national championship.

GLOSSARY

Anasazi

An ancient Native American culture that first appeared in New Mexico about 2,000 to 3,500 years ago. They built their homes in the sides of cliffs. Also called the Ancestral Puebloans.

Basin

A bowl-like dip in the Earth's surface.

Canyon

A deep, narrow river valley with steep sides.

Clovis Culture

A prehistoric Paleo-Indian culture that existed in New Mexico starting approximately 11,000 years ago. They used stone spear points to hunt big game such as mammoths and elk. They are named for the spear points that archeologists first discovered near the town of Clovis, New Mexico.

Conquistadors

Spanish soldiers and explorers who came to North and South America in the 1500s. They used force to conquer native people and take control of their lands.

Hispanic

A term that refers to people and cultures that are linked to Spain, especially lands that were once colonized by Spain, such as New Mexico.

IRRIGATION

Supplying water to dry land. In one method, rows of ditches are dug and filled with water that is diverted from nearby rivers. The water seeps into the ground, allowing plants to grow in previously unusable lands.

MESA

A hill or mountain with steep sides and a flat top.

NAVAJO

A group of Native Americans that live primarily in New Mexico, Arizona, and Utah. They are known for their work with livestock, as well as for creating beautiful weavings, pottery, and silver jewelry.

PETROLEUM

A thick, yellow-to-black, oily liquid found below the earth's surface. It is used to make gasoline, kerosene, heating oil, and many other products. When pumped from the ground, it is commonly called crude oil.

PLATEAU

An area of high, flat land.

POW-WOW

A Native American social gathering where the people dance, sing, and honor their culture. Pow-wows are sacred events. Many are private, but some are open for the public to observe. Large pow-wows may last an entire week.

RESERVOIR

A natural or man-made area for storing a large amount of water. Most reservoirs are created by building a dam on a river.

RODEO

A contest in which men and women athletes compete in events such as riding horses and bulls and catching cattle with lassos.

INDEX